2014 Annual

BEST IDEAS

★ ★ ★ ★ ★ ★ ★ ★

America in Bloom

Planting pride in our communities

Printed in USA by Createspace
ISBN-13: 978-1500927813
ISBN-10: 1500927813

America in Bloom envisions communities across the country as welcoming and vibrant places to live, work, and play—benefiting from colorful plants and trees; enjoying clean environments; celebrating heritage; and planting pride through volunteerism.

America in Bloom is a 501(c)(3) non-profit organization.

This book was made possible by volunteers.
Concept - Leslie Pittenger
Editing - Leslie Pittenger and Evelyn Alemanni
Design, layout, print coordination - Evelyn Alemanni

America in Bloom
2130 Stella Ct.
Columbus, OH 43215
614-487-1117   aib@AmericaInBloom.org
www.AmericaInBloom.org

America in Bloom   3

Printed in USA by Createspace
ISBN-13: 978-1500927813
ISBN-10: 1500927813

America in Bloom envisions communities across the country as welcoming and vibrant places to live, work, and play—benefiting from colorful plants and trees; enjoying clean environments; celebrating heritage; and planting pride through volunteerism.

America in Bloom is a 501(c)(3) non-profit organization.

This book was made possible by volunteers.
Concept - Leslie Pittenger
Editing - Leslie Pittenger and Evelyn Alemanni
Design, layout, print coordination - Evelyn Alemanni

America in Bloom
2130 Stella Ct.
Columbus, OH 43215
614-487-1117   aib@AmericaInBloom.org
www.AmericaInBloom.org

★ 2014 Annual ★

Contents

....

Cover images:

Top row: McCall, ID; Lexington, KY; Greendale, IN

Center row: Madisonville, KY; Pella, IA; University of Findlay, OH

Bottom row: Coshocton, OH; Arroyo Grande, CA

....

On the following pages, + indicates text from evaluations.

Where possible, images were selected to match the text; photos were limited to what participants and judges submitted.

★ ★ ★ ★ ★ ★ ★ ★

About America in Bloom

As we travel across America, some towns are more striking than others. They appear cleaner, prettier, more welcoming. We may feel comfortable in their ambiance without knowing exactly why. These are the places where we want to spend time, maybe even relocate there. Chances are these towns are some of the many America in Bloom (AIB) participants.

Our country is experiencing a resurgence of residents who want to be actively involved in their communities, addressing many urgent needs. America in Bloom is providing the framework to get the job done via its annual awards program.

Plan to participate in the America in Bloom program year after year for the boost it can give your town. Registration information is included on page 40. With America in Bloom you can dig in and plant pride in your city.

America in Bloom is a 501(c)(3) non-profit organization. Our board and judges are all volunteers.

The Best Ideas Book Series

The Best Ideas book series was conceived when one of the AIB judges realized the importance of sharing all the great ideas she was seeing in towns across the United States. There have been several editions, culminating in the *Ten Years of Best Ideas* published in 2012. That book offers more than 2000 best practices and photos and is arranged by evaluated criteria.

This annual update showcases the best ideas from 2014 AIB participants. It features best ideas submitted in their community profiles and in some cases, ideas selected from evaluations by the editors of this edition. Some of the text has been edited for space considerations. The Special Mentions were also excerpted from the evaluations and are the work of AIB judges.

If you don't yet own the Ten Years of Best Ideas book, you can order it at www.AmericaInBloom.org.

Additional copies of this addendum can also be ordered there as well.

We hope you enjoy the Best Ideas book and this addendum and find many useful ideas and programs for your town.

Gallipolis, OH

★ Arroyo Grande, CA

Special Mention: New Mural

Arroyo Grande's recently completed mural depicting early agricultural life in the town is an outstanding example of the potential power and beauty of public art. Highly detailed, yet large enough to be impactful, it is a real traffic stopper. The artist went to great pains to research for historic accuracy. Her success was evident when an elderly resident was reportedly moved to tears upon first viewing it because it brought back such strong memories.

Best Ideas: This is the first year that Arroyo Grande has included Public Art in our Community Profile. We believe that the integration of public art in communities supports the basic philosophy and ideals promoted by America in Bloom. At a minimum, Arroyo Grande's program contributes to the categories of Heritage Preservation and Overall Impression. The Arroyo Grande Public Art Program was started in 2013; as of March 2014, four projects are slated for near term city approval. We believe that the inclusion of public art to enhance the overall appearance and impression of cities and communities is extremely important. For these reasons, we are proud to promote this program as Arroyo Grande In Bloom's (AGIB) "Best Idea."

★ Bad Axe, Michigan

Special Mention: Entrance Signs

The entrance signs into Bad Axe are being improved with the help of volunteers and the organizations that sponsor the signs. The landscaping around the sign entering Bad Axe from the north on Rt 53 was recently improved just before the America In Bloom visit.

Best Ideas: We feel that the best thing we could do as a committee was to get the media behind the America in Bloom contest. We have a community newspaper with two of its employees on the committee, and they have graciously allowed the use of space for articles pertaining to all of the projects and contests that were coordinated by the group. We were able to get as much involvement in plantings as possible and had a greater number of participants in contests because the news was well distributed.

+One project planned by the Bad Axe America in Bloom committee is to host a number of contests among the community. One of them will be a "Best Dressed" Church contest and a "Best Dressed Business" contest. This will serve to improve the overall landscaping of the many churches and businesses that are located in Bad Axe as well as offer a little bit of friendly competition. The winners of the contests will win traveling trophies, free services (such as advertising), and contributions to their charity efforts. The Master Gardeners will host a garden walk to attract visitors to view the contest participants' offerings and vote for their favorites.

★ Belpre, Ohio

Special Mention: Historical Preservation of the Carriage

An 1840s C-Spring Boot Carriage built by the Brewster Carriage Company of Brewster, New York has been completely restored and is on display in the new addition at the museum. This is quite an acquisition for such a small town museum.

Best Ideas The use of an insert in the city water bills to inform the residents and businesses of the AIB judging date and other pertinent information was vital to the success of this year's program. The insert contained the designated "color" for the year, dates of judging, how to make a difference and volunteer. It also shared the link to our Facebook page where our progress is posted!

2013 was a year of sprucing up with paint and the best paint project is a very simple one, and involves upcycling. We collected old tires and distributed them to schools in Belpre. Art classes have been turning them vibrant colors, and high school students have even created designed "stacks". These will be used at parks and public areas as planters. A Girl Scout Troop is finishing the project by painting additional tires and designing the layout to be used in the parks. Recently a little boy walked into the city building with his father, and was so excited to see a tire he had helped paint! His excitement was enough to make us realize our tire painting project has involved kids in a new way, as they are able see their work shared all over town.

A committee member mentioned just recently that, if we were to call a halt to our participation in America in Bloom right now, we have already made such incredible progress in enhancing the natural beauty of our little town. The work has been a pleasure, and we continue to look forward to exciting new projects that will make our city even more pleasant place to live and work. America in Bloom has motivated and energized a whole new, talented group of volunteers, and for that we are already being rewarded.

Belpre in **Bloom**

2013
Outstanding Achievement Award
"Community Involvement"

2014 FLOWER COLOR IS PINK
PLEASE USE THIS COLOR IN YOUR YARD!

Judging by
America in Bloom
July 7th & 8th, 2014

Please join us in
"Planting Pride"

Community Wide
Beautification Week is
May 12th thru May 18th

Get out and make a difference!

TO VOLUNTEER CALL (740) 423-7592

Learn more here:
f facebook.com/belpreinbloom

★ Brewton, Alabama

Special Mention: Brewton Reborn

Brewton Reborn is a nine-month program welcoming municipal, business and residential participants to bring the community together while making small manageable improvements. This program was so successful that the community plans to do it again this year.

Best Ideas: Brewton Reborn - Brewton is just completing a nine-month project to build a strong sense of community through simple tasks and events that promote volunteerism, leadership and economic growth. The launch date was July 1, 2013.

Each month, city residents and neighbors are practicing three specific tasks. We started with these in July:

1) Leave your house. It's simple. Get outside. Join a civic group. Help with a service project. Be involved. If you need some ideas on groups looking for members, call city hall, Kiwanis, Rotary, Civitan, Lions, SWAG, Adopt-a-Block and the list goes on.

2) Pick up litter. If everyone in town picked up just one piece of litter a day that he or she didn't throw down, our town would be clean in a few weeks.

3) Know your neighbors. See that little house down the street? Go knock on the door and introduce yourself. We will focus on Friendly Fridays.

August: 1) Look up when you are walking. 2) Greet people. 3) Sit on your porch.

September: 1) Plant flowers. 2) Use your library. 3) Buy from local merchants.

October: 1) Garden together. 2) Support neighborhood schools. 3) Take children to the park.

November: 1) Fix it even if you didn't break it. 2) Have potlucks. 3) Honor elders.

December: 1) Turn off your TV. 2) Read stories aloud. 3) Talk to the mail carrier.

January: 1) Put up a swing. 2) Organize a block party. 3) Bake extra and share.

February: 1) Open your shades. 2) Turn up the music. 3) Listen before you react to anger.

March: 1) Mediate a conflict. 2) Seek to understand. 3) Learn from new and uncomfortable angles.

★ Calabasas, California

Calabasas has added three round-abouts to slow down traffic on the roads system through residential neighborhoods. Additional sites are currently being identified for implementation. These functional features are attractively landscaped to include night lighting. Community members along with the judges praise the city for their efforts.

Best Ideas: The best idea Calabasas had in 2013 was to revamp the focus points for a few sections within the city. These particular areas were in need of some landscape aesthetics and traffic safety implementations. The landscaping at the front entrance of a small community named The Calabasas Village Mobile Home Park was redesigned and includes a shuttle/bus stop shelter to beautify this once ailing entrance.

A section of road way on Park Sorrento within the Las Villas HOA Community was a problem area between local area residents and teen/bad behavioral drivers. This section of roadway is most utilized by residents and the community to frequent local area shopping centers in addition to being a "convenient" access road to travel from the east side of town to the west side of town and vice versa. Because these areas are seen daily by residents, the city believed they needed to be rehabilitated to keep the residents excited and happy to be living in such a beautiful city. The city completely updated the flowers, flower beds, and ground covers to beautify the areas. The city redid the landscaping in these areas to make them more aesthetically pleasing while addressing pedestrian safety at the same time.

+Residents can report potholes on the city's website and through the newly introduced smartphone application "Calabasas Connect" by submitting a request. Residents can also call City Hall or submit an electronic Citizen's Request on the city website letting the city know where an area needs graffiti removal or pot-hole maintenance.

Castle Rock, Washington

Special Mention: Jackson Hole

This well done project to clean up an eyesore by creating a bioswale/retention pond in the middle of downtown was led by biology teacher Ryan Penner. Numerous volunteers of all ages joined in the effort with equipment, planting, and cleanup.

Best Ideas: Joining America in Bloom was most likely the 'BEST IDEA' members of the Chamber of Commerce and the Mayor/City Council initiated during our inaugural year of 2012. The creation of the Castle Rock Community Development Alliance (CRCDA) and the ongoing activity of the Board of Directors in 2013 have propelled Castle Rock into the bright lights of a radiant future. Both capture the enthusiasm and energy of Castle Rock's incredible citizen volunteers and partnership with the civic and business leadership.

Empty and outdated storefront display - Castle Rock has several downtown storefronts that are merely used for storage by their owners. Some never intend to open a business, or offer the space for one. Many have occupied the same building for generations and the outdated interior space is visible to those passing on the street. Castle Rock America in Bloom (CR-AIB) proposed to the building owners that CR-AIB put seasonal planters in front of those 'empty' storefronts and where possible, provide and/or create attractive, seasonal displays. This has been well received by the business owners as well as the residents who walk, bike, drive, and shop along Castle Rock's main downtown business street.

+Castle Rock residents are beginning to catch the 'floral fever' and there are many neighborhoods where hanging baskets, flower gardens and container displays are evident. The CR-AIB 'Bloom Team' volunteers, in association with Windermere Realtors Community Service Day 2013, helped landscape eight homes for families participating in a 'self-help housing' program. A local nursery donated bedding plants and CR-AIB provided all eight families with a flowering container as a 'Welcome to Castle Rock' gift.

★ Catskill, New York

Special Mention: Renovation of Walkways

The walkways, or slides, that bring residents from the streets above to Main Street have been redone. Once a plain walkway is now filled with beautiful annuals and perennials and enjoyed by all. The container gardens on both the Howard Street and Mott Street slides are wonderful examples of properly crafted container garden from top to bottom that are outstanding.

Best Ideas: Our best idea is to continue what we are doing with Cultivate Catskill – to make it a coordination entity for the village for any improvements in the future. Our goals are to establish maintenance solutions for our watering and general clean-up of our streets and parks. We are still hoping to interest more individuals to be prideful in our community and to join our forces to make all this one concerted effort for improvement of our Village of Catskill.

★ Coshocton, Ohio

Special Mention: Planters on Main St. and Courthouse Square.

This year, the Coshocton is Blooming committee received grants for the purchase of large, exquisite containers that complement the color and architecture of the court-house. They have been placed around the courthouse square and beyond in the downtown area and planted with this year's signature red annuals. Soon businesses will be able to "rent" them for the season and have the CiB committee plant and maintain them.

Best Ideas: As we reflect back upon these past four years, it is obvious that our best idea has been to participate in the annual America in Bloom national competi-tion and to create Coshocton is Blooming as a new community organization to spon-sor and carry forward that effort. But even that idea has been significantly enhanced by the decision to continue to participate each year since the first. In fact, we have never stopped preparing for the next judges' visit. America in Bloom and Coshocton is Blooming have very simply become a part of the fabric of our community. Encouraged by this program, we have worked together to build community confidence and pride around the America in Bloom program on a continuing, year-round basis. No story more clearly exemplifies the result than the on-going work to establish a true urban forestry program for the City of Coshocton. The magnitude of change is huge, and it is ALL the result of the AIB evaluation and the encouragement and credibility it provided for a small group of people to accomplish a great deal. We are a work in progress.

+In 2013, the Pomerene Center for the Arts worked with New York City's Vamos architects to create the world's first Root Ball Park. The root balls of nineteen trees were transformed into bean bags, and placed at the three high schools in the community. When the school season was over, the trees were transported to the park space south of the courthouse square. When the project was completed, these trees were planted by the city in public sites around the community.

★ Echo, Oregon

Special Mention: Downtown Art

The city is beginning a new project to incorporate more artwork in downtown. They are off to a good start with the incorporation of art objects in some of the downtown planters. This project is sure to blossom just as other initiatives have been successful in the recent past.

Best Ideas: The Downtown Plan (renovation of downtown) is the best idea in decades. The improvements blend with commercial improvements-particularly the Koontz Building Renovation. The historic ambience remains while custom improvements such as benches, street lights, planters, bike racks, etc. make it uniquely Echo in style. It is also a project that not only Echo residents, but visitors from other towns have been excited about and our donations for America in Bloom projects increased as a result.

+Perennial Guide. In 2013 a committee member put together a guide to perennials that do well in Echo. The guide was printed June 2014 and will be available for residents to check out at the library. It will also be placed on the city's website. We have also added articles in the newsletter with xeriscape information and lists of hardy plants.

+Beautification Contest. The city has continued the beautification contest started in 2006. Prizes are awarded to the "Top Ten" in Echo in Bloom for Floral Displays and Curb Appeal. We also recognize people on an honorable mention list and 2-3 residences for most improved. Awards included gift certificates, plants, garden books and garden art objects. Plaques recognizing winners are on display at city hall.

Between city hall and the museum is a floral display that adds whimsy, heritage and plenty of color

★ Estes Park, Colorado

Special Mention: Turf

The turf in Estes Park for both the municipal and commercial sectors is impeccable. 99.5% of the turf the judges viewed was completely weed-free, thick and healthy. It was an invitation to take off your shoes and walk through the grass. There was absolutely no grass growing in the cracks of the city sidewalks. Under the guidance of Tonya Ziegler the program that the city is using is working extremely well. Areas without turf have been taken to their natural state using native grasses and wildflowers.

Best Ideas: +The community is pursuing a Creative Arts District designation. One component of this is incorporating landscaped areas and art in public spaces. This brings to the forefront the many types of art in the Estes Valley area, including floral and landscaping.

The Parks Department partnered with the Estes Park Tree Board and the Bureau of Reclamation to construct the habitat enclosure/bird sanctuary on the 9-hole golf course. The enclosure protects the area and its valuable bird habitat and nesting area from bull elk, which can be very destructive as they rub their antlers on trees and other vegetation. The natural-looking fence blends with the area and has ensured the successful regeneration of the habitat and its vegetation.

Solar rebates available through the Town of Estes Park and the Colorado Governor's Energy Office also made it easier for residents to install solar panels at their homes. In 2009, six residents won a lottery to participate in the program. After asking one resident how much he spends on utilities after the installation, he said with a smile, "About $6 a month." Solar even powers trash compactors in downtown Estes Park.

★ Fayetteville, Arkansas

Special Mention: Wastewater Facility

The Wastewater Facility utilizes a process (biosolids) reducing waste and producing safe, organic material for fertilization meeting EPA regulations for Class A Exceptional Quality. It's safe for commercial/residential application. A solar process incorporating a secondary thermal drying process makes Fayetteville's the only community undertaking this process in the United States.

Best Ideas: The Environmental Action Committee (EAC) set a goal of being the first community in Arkansas to become a Certified Wildlife Habitat by the National Wildlife Federation. To date, eight schools are certified. At several there was a whole school assembly where the mayor presented the certificate and the EAC members presented a habitat kit to improve the schools' efforts.

+The local AIB Committee formed a partnership with Fayetteville police and firefighters and Woodland Junior High students to make a special product, Taginator, available for residents if they are victims of graffiti. Wal-Mart made a donation of a pressure cleaner and water supply to help remove graffiti from public property.

+An Urban Forester visited the high school and discussed urban forestry, tree benefits, and tree preservation with high school students through the first annual Fayetteville High School Outdoor Recreation Classroom. The Urban Forestry Program also shared educational press and articles on the following topics: Invasive Species Awareness Week (NISAW), Tree Care During Drought Conditions, and local native and invasive plants.

★ Gallipolis, Ohio

Special Mention: Gallipolis River Front Welcome Sign

The Gallipolis River Front Welcome Sign focuses on the importance of the Ohio River as one of the great assets of Gallipolis - for its beauty and the opportunity for economic growth it offers from fishing, boating and tourism. The artistic quality of this elegant new sign sets a precedent for the kind of quality development anticipated for the Gallipolis Riverfront.

Best Ideas: Our "Best Idea" implemented in 2014 sponsored by Gallipolis in Bloom (GIB) has been the Community Garden. On land donated by an area business, five raised beds were constructed by Boy Scout Troop #200. It was filled with organic compost and peat moss by the Boy Scouts and members of GIB. Over 50 Washington Elementary students enrolled in the after school program for ages 5-12 and planted 50 dozen seeds in egg cartons. They then transplanted the seedlings into a raised bed donated by the PTO at the dedication ceremony on May 1. This is an organic garden with no chemical pesticides or fertilizers allowed. It is free to any individual or group that desires to plant an organic garden. Water is supplied by a rain barrel system donated by the Gallia Soil and Water Conservation District. The rain barrel is attached to a garage next door to the donated property. Although we are starting small this year, future plans include additional beds for next year, including a handicap accessible bed for seniors, or a handicapped individual. A survey of empty lots in the city has been completed, and we hope to further expand into other areas of the city with additional community garden areas.

A new 40 foot welcome sign located at the Riverfront area was dedicated on April 25. This sign depicts the Founding French men and women who came to live here in 1790 and features the Fleur de Lis that symbolizes our city. Along with the four new containers of flowers that spell out OHIO, river travelers now know exactly where they are when they are cruising on the Ohio River. This welcome sign was a recommendation for our first set of America in Bloom judges in 2006. We have talked about this sign for years, but did not have the resources to undertake such a project. Last summer, the Retail Merchants security group approached the Gallipolis in Bloom committee and asked us to head up the project and they would fund it. A local artist designed the sign and contracted with the other local experts to get it built. This is certainly a stamp that Gallipolis in Bloom has left for the community.

★ Greendale, Indiana

Special Mention: Dearborn County Recycling Center

The Dearborn County Recycling Center provides recycled office and craft supplies to Greendale and anyone in the surrounding communities. There is a room filled with prom dresses and another with costumes so that those not able to afford these items can still participate. The Green Garden is created out of all recycled materials and is a great example of repurposing items that would normally be tossed into a landfill.

Best Ideas: We are proud and grateful for our ten years of participation in the America In Bloom program. We pore over our evaluation each year and earmark recommendations we consider a good fit for our community, implementing those recommendations as resources permit. It is understatement to say AIB has helped us grow.

One of the suggestions from our 2013 America in Bloom judges was to print a companion piece to our Community Tree Guide in order to advise residents on the selection of shrubs and perennials that attract pollinators. Taking that great idea from the judges, we made it our own by including shrubs and perennials that Bambi won't want to dine on. It's an important consideration in an area where the deer population is a real problem for homeowners.

+Residents are encouraged to "Nominate a Neighbor" for recognition of their landscaping efforts by the Garden Club. Forms are available at the Utility Building and through Garden Club members. Nominees are listed on the Garden Club's website and receive a certificate of appreciation and recognition at the annual autumn appreciation dinner.

+We continue our on-going program to mount benches, tables, and trash receptacles on concrete slabs in parks. This reduces mowing and weed eating issues and makes for a neater appearance. This has been in response to an AIB judge's suggestion and it's some of the best advice we've been given.

★ Henderson County, North Carolina

Special Mention: Hendersonville Main Street Renovation

The completion of the Hendersonville Main Street renovation is very well received by the residents, tourists, and businesses. The result is a model for the entire country. Few communities have such a well-designed gem in downtown. Hundreds of small communities would love to have such a beautiful Main Street. All of Henderson County will benefit from this excellent project.

Best Ideas: The Park at Flat Rock was acquired in the fall of 2013. Originally an 18-hole golf course, the park is currently under restoration. When complete, the 64-acre park will include a 1.5 mile perimeter loop and an additional 1.3 miles of secondary trails. Additional phases of park amenities will include picnic and pavilion areas, children's playgrounds, and an outdoor amphitheater. The long-term master plan for the 66-acre Park at Flat Rock will involve converting meadows, streams and wetlands into trails, playgrounds, and open spaces for the public to enjoy. Initial priorities include the completion of a 1.5-mile perimeter trail, installation of benches, restrooms and a picnic pavilion. Future amenities may include a new entrance and parking lot, playgrounds, and an interpretive area in the wetlands as an education component.

Hendersonville's major project in 2013 was the completion of infrastructure renovations on Main Street. In the late 1970s, Hendersonville's Main Street was changed from a wide four-lane configuration to a serpentine pattern. In the 30+years since that transformation, some of the original features became outdated, storm drains were failing, electrical outlets retrofitted for street festivals were unsafe, and some street trees were dying. These problems led to plans for a complete renovation. The work of tearing up the streets and sidewalks was painful for visitors and merchants alike; however, after much thought, the City Council determined to go ahead and finish the project. The final result has exceeded all expectations. Although common themes run the entire length, each block has its own personality. The final result is a downtown which everyone can enjoy and be proud of.

★ Holland, Michigan

Special Mention: Three-Volume History of Holland

Holland, Michigan: From Dutch Colony to Dynamic City - the first comprehensive history of Holland, is being released in a three-volume set. Written over a 10-year period by Robert P. Swierenga, publication was made possible by the Van Raalte Institute and their colleagues.

Best Ideas: The Macatawa Watershed is a 175-square mile watershed including Lake Macatawa, the Macatawa River, and nearly 700 miles of rivers, streams and ditches. Lake Macatawa, formerly known as Black Lake, was once a clear lake (called Black Lake because of the tannins and dead leaf matter that coated the bottom of the lake, giving the lake a black appearance.) Its shores reach the City of Holland and is a destination for visitors throughout the summer season. The lake offers fishing, watersports and boating playing a critical role in Holland's tourism.

In March of 2011, an 18 month study began to determine the exact source of the sediment, nutrient, and bacterial pollution plaguing the Macatawa Watershed. The organizers of the study included the Outdoor Discovery Center Macatawa Greenway, Macatawa Area Coordinating Council, and Hope College, with help from Grand Valley State University's Annis Water Resources Institute and Michigan State University. The collaborative effort was privately funded and was considered Phase One of a multi-year research and restoration project. With the results in hand from Phase One research, a team of water quality experts developed a three-part approach to address the identified issues, including:

1. Wetland Restoration and Engineered Water Quality solutions
2. Water Quality Best Management Practices implementation in Urban and Agricultural areas
3. Community Information and Education about the issues impacting water quality within the Macatawa Watershed.

Please see www.macatawaclarity.org for an exciting video and updated information.

★ Holliston, Massachusetts

Special Mention: Moving a Large Stone Wall

Holliston in Bloom is an incredibly hard working group. They not only work on beautification projects but see other challenges in their community and tackle them. They are moving a large stone wall between buildings to connect parking with downtown shops. This effort involves numerous people and they developed signage to alert residents.

Best Ideas: Our take-away from the America in Bloom symposium in 2012 was "welcoming spaces." We applied a design-eye to an inventory of town spaces and thus, created small places where people can stop and rest, chat, eat lunch or just pass by and feel good about the way the spaces look. We've added planters to the landing at the front of Town Hall and along the sides of benches located downtown. We've worked with the library to update their space a bit by significantly lowering the hedge in the front and adding a second bench for reading. We added a gazebo to Gooch's corner. We have created a patio on the side of Town Hall for employees and residents to sit. We are working to add a second Welcome to Holliston sign soon. We have AIB to thank for these ideas. All of these steps are taken in response to what we learned from year one in AIB.

+The Holliston Garden Club (HGC) has a group called *The Treespotters* who look for trees that are unusual so as to educate both the membership and the community at-large. The members identified specific trees and researched them for the Holliston Garden Club Tree of the Month Articles sent to members and posted on the web site. They worked with the town liaison at the golf course, and HGC identified the major trees on the course. Trees were researched, and identified with photographs. Signs and a poster were designed to be hung in the club house and laminated placemats to be used in the restaurant. The restaurant paid for the placemats and the golf course paid for the three foot poster. Included in the poster were little known facts about the trees. For example, the shagbark hickory tree is used to produce drumsticks and to smoke bacon. HGC hoped that people, while dining or golfing, including the young golfers, would absorb information about the trees growing in Holliston.

★ Lewisburg, West Virginia

Special Mention: "Garden Space" Pocket Park

Challenged with keeping their historic downtown vibrant and active, Lewisburg made a courageous decision to build a beautiful pocket park along its main street with lawn, trees and a bronze statue. To this park they added a small on grade fountain that is a huge hit with families. Children are laughing and playing in this fountain all summer long. It is a model of just how small an interactive fountain can be to bring vitality to a downtown.

Best Ideas: Transforming the former dilapidated Fort Savannah Inn property in Lewisburg's Historic District into a community park now known as Montwell Park.

Montwell Park is an ambitious and encompassing project transforming the northern entrance to downtown Lewisburg. Plans for the park began with the purchase of the former Fort Savannah Inn property. Four acres of historic land surrounding the Inn was generously donated by a local family with the stipulation that it remains park land for the community to enjoy.

Greenbrier Valley Restoration Project (GVRP) is a non-profit organization founded to create and govern Montwell Park. GVRP's purpose is to build and govern Montwell Park to enhance the quality of life for Greenbrier Valley residents and create synergy in the elements that will occupy the park, including gardens, market pavilion, youth center, farm-to-table restaurant and community meeting space.

As a first step in developing the park, GVRP needed to remove two condemned motel buildings on the property. As a powerful signal of its support for the long-term project, the City of Lewisburg contributed $165,000 toward the buildings' demolition, as well as important water management improvements. Next, the existing log building was extensively renovated, which included installing a new roof to fire code, reinforcing the main floor, installing a new kitchen and updating the water system. The log buildings upper floor now houses a non-profit farm-to-table restaurant and community event space. A youth center will occupy the lower level. Montwell Park will be developed over time to include a pavilion building for a farmers market and other functions, plus gardens, walking trails, and a pond. It will be open for all to enjoy and we anticipate that it will help attract more visitors to Greenbrier County.

★ Lexington, Kentucky

Special Mention: The Urban Boundary

The Urban Boundary created in 1958 continues to protect the city's culture, history, and agricultural lands from urban sprawl and define the city's character. A Purchase of Development Rights program spearheaded by Fayette Alliance has saved 27,000 acres from development. This program assures that owners of agricultural lands are kept whole in exchange for not selling their land for more dense development.

Best Ideas: +The Grow Again Garden at Cardinal Hill Rehabilitation Hospital is actively used in patients' therapy and is a restful place for patients to visit with their families. Patients, many of whom have gardens at home, enjoy caring for the beds, from planting through harvesting. They help maintain and replenish the flower beds throughout the growing season so plants are always in bloom. A popular patient therapy activity is cutting flowers to take back to their rooms.

FAYETTE COUNTY PUBLIC SCHOOLS (FCPS) has adopted a no idling policy for school buses to limit harmful emissions on school campuses and have partnered with KY Division for Air Quality to pilot a student-driven no idling automobile policy in eight schools. To implement, students collect pre-campaign data, raise awareness through newsletters, posters, permanent signs and announcements and collect post-campaign data. Participating parents are incentivized with car decals, key chains, pencils etc.

SEEDS (Service Education and Entrepreneurship in Downtown Spaces) - SEEDS is a summer youth program sponsored by Seedleaf. It targets 5th – 11th grade students living in areas of Lexington that have been identified as food deserts. In an attempt to connect these youth with healthy fresh food, participants are involved in all aspects of growing food in an urban setting. Students gain hands-on experience in growing and caring for a garden, meal preparation, and nutrition basics. Participants also learn the fundamentals of entrepreneurship as they work to develop a business venture that involves selling their healthy products in their community. The goal of this project is to help young Lexingtonians become healthy food ambassadors in their community.

★ Madisonville, Kentucky

Special Mention: "Growing Warriors"

One group that will have a presence in Madisonville's Mahr Park will be "Growing Warriors." The mission of this group is "To Equip, Assist, and Train our military veterans with the skills they need to produce high quality organically grown produce for their families and communities." Not only is this venture healing minds and bodies, but it increases self-esteem as it teaches survival skills in today's world.

Best Ideas: Through the Mahr Park at Hidden Hills Farm, the City of Madisonville is partnering with a cutting edge organization called Growing Warriors. The Growing Warriors Project is a program that is designed to train, assist, and equip veteran families with the skills, tools, and supplies needed to grow high quality, naturally grown produce for their families, their communities, and their country. Currently, plans are to begin the project during the summer of 2014 with soil testing, soil preparation, and fencing. A grant has already been secured from the US Department of Agriculture to grow a specialty crop. During the fall of 2014, 500 blueberry bushes will be planted as the first crop for the project. Plans to expand include vegetable gardens, a community garden, and even an orchard. Areas for small "community gardens" will be designated for approximately 30 families to grow produce, with room to expand as participants register and funding is provided. These garden plots will be for veteran and low income families. Training and support will be provided by veterans. Through the Growing Warriors Project, veterans in Madisonville will be able to work on a farm that is producing food to feed families, supply a food bank, or be sold at the Farmer's Market. The veterans and community will have the opportunity to come together to share in monthly classes that will teach sustainable agricultural techniques, how to grow organic food, and other farming concepts. Side by side, veterans will be able to work with local community volunteers and organizations to grow the crops from "seed to plate." For more information, visit www.growingwarriors.org

★ McCall, Idaho

Special Mention: Centennial Plaza

An artistically designed and well executed wall and landscape was recently completed to commemorate the 100th Anniversary of McCall. Mosaics lead the viewer on a history of McCall and significant events in the country. An interpretive plaque will soon be installed to complete the excellent project.

Best Ideas: For many years, residents and visitors of McCall have identified the need for a system of connected sidewalks and pathways in the community. McCall is an active, recreation based community, and the city has worked hard toward improving its pathway network for pedestrians and bicyclists.

The Third Street Corridor is the main commercial corridor in McCall. In 2011, the city applied for and was granted funding from the Idaho Department of Commerce to address infrastructure deficiencies in the area. The Community Development Block Grant (Housing and Urban Development) of $494,400 was combined with municipal and private partner funding to design, engineer, and construct two blocks of curb, gutter, sidewalk, bike lanes, street trees, light poles, and water/sewer/stormwater improvements. The project began construction in November, 2012, and was completed in November, 2013.

The total project cost was $1.1 million, but the benefit to the community far outweighs the financial cost. Businesses that were isolated from the downtown core are now connected. Pedestrians and bicyclists can safely access services, businesses and recreational sites. Payette Lake water quality (source of city's drinking water) is improved by new stormwater filtering. Businesses and residents benefit from improved water and sewer services, and fire flows are improved. The corridor is attractive, well lit, appropriately signed, and parking is improved. There are additional light poles and the city's hanging basket program has been expanded. The McCall Improvement Committee (AIB Committee) is sponsoring a banner program to help enhance the corridor with colorful "McCall in Bloom" banners.

★ Morro Bay, California

Special Mention: Guerilla Gardeners Garden Club

The Guerilla Gardeners Garden Club runs a zero waste program to educate and assist other organizations of all kinds to reduce landfill demand and focus on recycling and reuse. They also provide plants and labor to enhance various areas. They make a substantial difference.

Best Ideas: Unlike most other volunteer groups in Morro Bay, Morro Bay in Bloom organizes brief project activities on a weekly basis. Morro Bay in Bloom has also made a commitment to the Surfboard Art Festival as a means of raising awareness of the impact of public art in well-maintained public spaces, but our best idea is bringing volunteers together frequently over time.

Our aim is to encourage "ownership" of the city by its citizens. We believe that by working side by side with someone you didn't know very well before helps to build ties beyond the usual relationships. And when you see a project you worked on begin to take hold, it fosters a feeling of pride and of being part of the whole community. These attitudes will generalize; Morro Bay in Bloom volunteers will start seeing things in the public domain they ignored before and take responsibility for them.

We are determined to keep Morro Bay in Bloom a "politics free zone" where we focus on what we have in common. Over time, we plan to grow our volunteer base and expand our collaboration with like-minded people in other groups. There is no room for competition in these projects – there's more than enough for all of us to do!

+Water conservation techniques that will be followed include: maintain existing plants at a minimal level, but ensure the survival of trees. Mulch deeply to conserve soil moisture, replace thirsty plants with drought-tolerant ones that grow well in our area. Remove turf and replace it with less thirsty plants and/ or hardscape, keep planted areas totally free of water competition from weeds and invasive overgrowth. Allow plants that can tolerate it to die back until more water is available and choose landscaping designs that incorporate a lot of open area for rock, hardscape, mulch and urban art displays.

★ Ottawa, Illinois

Special Mention: Youth Art Initiative

Youth are very active in the creation of art that is publically and permanently displayed in Ottawa in a number of venues. On an ongoing basis at the farmer's market a booth full of mosaic pieces invites children to assemble free-of-charge a mosaic of their own design that is then applied by volunteers to otherwise plain trash cans in the downtown area. The use of mosaic as a design medium has particular meaning as it speaks to Ottawa's history as an early glass and marble manufacturing center. On one weekend children were also invited to decorate numerous picnic tables in Allen Park with symbols and their handprints. They decorated the walls of both the men's and women's restrooms with colorful designs and symbols. A mural was added to the outside of the structure by the participants.

Best Ideas: +To ease the concerns of potential gardening volunteers who are not expert gardeners, the City of Ottawa created a "Volunteer Gardener Handbook" which outlines the basic responsibilities of the volunteers along with the many benefits to Ottawa of their work.

To further brighten Ottawa, the Ottawa Is Blooming Committee partnered with the Ottawa Garden Club to make 2014 the Year of the Zinnia. This has resulted in thousands of zinnias planted across downtown Ottawa and the rest of the city.

The Ottawa Tree Board has held an annual "Suds for Saplings" fundraiser – a beer tasting event co-sponsored by a local liquor store – on Arbor Day to raise funds to plant dozens of trees across the City of Ottawa with special focus on the city parks. This year, the event will be held in late June and has been renamed "Brews, Buds and Blooms" as the proceeds were shared with the Ottawa is Blooming Committee to help finance the City of Ottawa's entry in the America In Bloom awards program.

★ Pella, Iowa

Special Mention: Tulip Displays

Pella is known for its tulip displays, which peak in early May each year. Volunteers from the local college, schools, and businesses work alongside city staff and volunteer residents to plant over 200,000 bulbs each fall. Later, after the tulips have flowered, volunteers help remove the bulbs and prepare the sites for summer plantings.

Best Ideas: Incorporated storm water runoff collection at the new Pella Sports Park to be used for irrigation. The collection of storm water helps reduce runoff and reduces the need for city water to keep the sports fields in good playing condition.

+Pella Community Middle School received a grant to install an additional water bottle filling station near their lunch room. The grant proposal submitted by 8th graders, stated, "We would like to gain another one of these water fountains for many reasons. It eliminates plastic water bottle waste, and if we had one of these fountains for a whole year, based on the information we have, it would save nearly 6,000 bottles!" In November 2013 a follow up report submitted by Josh Manning, Middle School Principal, stated they have saved almost 1,400 water bottles in the first 3 months alone.

+Memorial Trees can be purchased through the Community Services Center. The program has recently been revised to better incorporate trees into the city's overall plan. Tree species and locations are identified for selection. This ensures that the appropriate trees are placed in the right location for the right purpose. Plaques are included and can be personalized to recognize individuals or special events.

★ Portsmouth, Ohio

Special Mention: Loan of Flower Pots

Portsmouth Main Street Good Neighbor offered businesses the pledge of a loan of flower pots for the good faith pledge to:
- Keep the flowers watered
- Keep the front of their business clean by picking up trash and pulling weeds.

Businesses responded with support for 40 flower pots, 12 window boxes, and 27 hanging baskets.

Best Ideas: This year we implemented the Main Street Portsmouth Boneyfiddle Good Neighbor Pledge. We purchased 40 black flower pots and 12 black window boxes. We offered to loan these to businesses who agree to sign our pledge. The pledge states that in exchange for the use of the flower pots and window boxes they will keep them watered and keep the front of their business clean by picking up the trash and pulling weeds.

So far we have had a tremendous response. Everyone was excited to receive the flower pots and boxes. Business owners are taking an interest in the appearance of the outside of their store fronts and have been out cleaning. This has been a tremendous issue in our downtown. Hopefully, it will continue throughout the year.

On the Chillicothe Street business district we purchased 27 hanging baskets at $250.00 each. The basket frames were fabricated locally. The baskets have 2 gallon water reservoir which makes them much easier to care for.

In the past we have not received much support from that district and limited our work to The Esplanade and the 4th and 7th Street Municipal Parking lots. Initially we were approached by a business owner on Chillicothe Street who asked about the baskets that were added to Market Street. He personally went up and down the street asking for sponsors. So far, 22 baskets have been sponsored. We are amazed by the compliments we have received and this is the most response we have ever received from social media.

★ Racine, Wisconsin

Special Mention: Prairie School water testing program

This project educates children and creates a volunteer network which monitors local stream and river health, shares data for educational purposes, and builds partnerships with resource protection programs within the Wind Point Watershed. Students and teachers collect water quality data and collaborate with the Wisconsin Department of Natural Resources and other agencies.

Best Ideas: Beauty in Our Community – Recognizing Positive Beautification Efforts. The program was started as a way to involve as many people as possible in beautifying the entire community. It was designed to recognize individuals for their efforts in beautifying their property, whether on the judges' tour route or not.

A recognition letter was mailed to each address that was nominated, either by a friend, a neighbor, or a city official. They also received a ballot that they could mail back to recognize someone else. The winner was drawn from the hundreds of ballots that had been mailed in over the previous few months, and received a hand-made gift at our Judges' Welcome Ceremony. The judges were present and were introduced along with other city officials. This was a highly motivating effort for the entire community. AIB has been a great marketing tool, and so popular that we plan to do it every year!

+Residents throughout Greater Racine are recognized for floral displays with an individual "Beauty in Our Community" certificate. Over 500 have been distributed in the last two years and have resulted in increased pride and beautification efforts.

★ Rockford, Illinois

Special Mention: Adaptive reuse of the Prairie Street Brew House

This is a prime example of how state and federal tax credits can be leveraged to create a variety of vibrant new facilities (multiple restaurants, residences, office space, event space, and brewery). Our commendations to the owners, developer, contractors, and architect for their vision and persistence in completing this welcome addition to Rockford's riverfront.

Best Ideas: +The fabric of any community is its neighborhoods and Rockford is fortunate to have extremely strong neighborhood organizations. In an effort to strengthen the neighborhood communities, a group of city officials and community leaders have once again banded to further an association of neighborhood groups called the Neighborhood Network. The network's aim is to identify emerging neighborhood organizations and rejuvenate existing ones through a variety of education and support opportunities. Promoting neighborhood pride and community involvement has been the focus of the America in Bloom effort, and as a result, an unusually high number of neighborhood clean-ups were held this spring. In April, "Keep Northern Illinois Beautiful" coordinated a community-wide clean-up. Additionally, more than 500 individuals along with several business partners took part in one of the largest clean-up projects ever through an annual cleanup called Earthbeat. The community received thousands of hours of free community service as a result of that effort.

Life is full of occasions to celebrate – weddings, births, anniversaries, the lives of loved ones lost. The Rockford Park District Foundations' Celebrate Life program offers people the opportunity for recognition of those moments with the gift of a tree or bench for placement in our communities' parks or golf courses. A plaque inscribed with the wording of the donor's choice accompanies each gift. In addition, a portion of each donation is set aside permanently to provide even more trees, benches, and other amenities for our parks in the future.

★ Santa Paula, California

Special Mention: Santa Paula Farm Worker Monument

This monument acknowledges the legacy of agriculture in America as represented historically by many ethnic and racial groups who came to this country seeking a better life. It is the only monument in the United States dedicated to the labor of farm workers.

Best Ideas: The city of Santa Paula and its America in Bloom committee have joined ranks to complete several projects. The city completed Las Piedras and Harding Park renovations and the American in Bloom committee completed the downtown expansion of floral displays.

Santa Paula is committed to offer our youth recreation areas that are well groomed and safe. Each weekend finds our parks filled with families attending sporting events or having family celebrations. Las Piedras Park is in a poor area of the city. Using CDBG and Development Impact fees, a million dollars went into improvements for Las Piedras. A new soccer field, irrigation system, athletic field lighting, basketball courts and landscaping renovated that area. The America in Bloom committee agreed to put final touches on the police substation building in the park as well.

America in Bloom Santa Paula (AIBSP) is in constant communication with the city and we agreed to expand the floral displays in the downtown area while the city was working on the parks. DoRight's Plant Growers manufactured the pole brackets at a much more reasonable price than we could purchase elsewhere and the city installed them on Mill Street, Santa Barbara Street and further east and west on Main Street. The floral corridor is now done and embellishes the historic center of town. Individual citizens, businesses and organizations have purchased memorial or honorarium placards at 28 locations so far. Visitors and citizens alike are often seen with cameras flashing. We are very proud that AIBSP and the city of Santa Paula's partnership has deepened through the years. Santa Paula has always been keenly aware of the need for renewal and renovation. AIBSP has been the key that the city uses to help achieve that renewal.

★ Slippery Rock, Pennsylvania

Special Mention: Macoskey Center

At the Macoskey Center, a 1920s farm has been transformed into a remarkable center of sustainability by the University of Slippery Rock for its students and the community. Permaculture farming techniques, solar and wind, reuse of construction products and a butterfly garden planted with the "lasagna process" all come together in this innovative hands on learning environment.

Best Ideas: Slippery Rock in Bloom (SRIB) discovered that not everyone owned a recycling receptacle and thus were not recycling at all. Recycling was a voluntary activity for the residents who wanted to participate. A "Recycling Receptacle at Every Home" initiative began in 2011. Local high school students, Sustainable Enterprise Accelerator faculty and students, and members of Slippery Rock in Bloom worked with the Butler County Recycling and Waste Management director to see what Slippery Rock in Bloom could do to provide receptacles for town and township residents. Through a state grant, SRIB was able to purchase receptacles for town and township residents. The high school students and SRIB members began a distribution project that included handing out rectangular receptacles at a local supermarket, Village Fest, and through the township municipal building. The next step was to provide recycling receptacles that had wheels that could be taken to the curb with ease. Beginning in fall 2013, each homeowner was provided a 50 gallon container with wheels.

Keystone Ridge Designs, a company that produces American made trash and recycling receptacles has met with SRIB and community leaders to design two traditional recycling cans. The receptacles will be placed near Gateway Park and on Main Street.

★ University of Findlay

Special Mention: "Hoop House Project"

Developed by Findlay Green Campus Initiative, the "Hoop House Project" is an innovative amalgam of community garden/organic vegetable production/incubator business. Students, professors and staff join together to produce organic food – in raised beds and on grade plots outside as well as under a greenhouse inside - and then share their harvest through CSA memberships of $200.

Best Ideas: In September 2013, the Green Campus Initiative teamed up with OilerWELL (employee wellness program) to offer a "Green Walk" on campus over the lunch hour. The purpose was twofold: to encourage employees to exercise and to familiarize our staff with the various environmental projects occurring on campus. Walkers met in front of Old Main and were given a map. Along the route, green balloons marked stopping points to learn about environmental efforts, including various recycling stations, sensory garden/retention pond, rain garden and the new Davis Street Addition. Thanks to a beautiful fall day and several volunteers, the walk was successful in educating our own staff about the role UF plays in local environmental efforts.

+Perhaps the longest running (2008) and most successful effort is "Recycle-Cycle," a bike lending and maintenance program that has provided from 15-25 reconditioned bicycles to UF students each semester. "Recycle-Cycle" boasts the following benefits: 1. Cost effective 2. Work-study employment for students 3. Improving campus environment 4. Reducing dependency on automobiles.

Since the program began, the campus has shown a remarkable gain in bicycle usage. The number of bike racks has increased by more than 30 percent in the past two years as a result of bike overflow in front of major classroom buildings. This is a campus that has sufficient parking spaces and does not charge for parking!

★ Venice, Florida

Special Mention: West Blalock Park

This park has been designated by the city as an arboretum. Its goal is to display and disseminate information about trees that will flourish in the Venice area. Venice's arboretum educates residents on tree ordinances, selection of appropriate trees for the home landscape, and the best care tasks.

Best Ideas: The city has two types of parks maintenance: county-maintained under the inter-local agreement and city-maintained. The county has various maintenance duties at 11 locations as outlined in the agreement. The city and county staffs meet quarterly at each site to review the condition of all facilities and amenities on these sites and note additional items that need attention, as well as any capital items that are the responsibility of the city. A spreadsheet is used to keep up with regular maintenance and duties. Without a schedule and designated duties for departments, maintenance would be much harder.

Some maintenance activities are; restrooms (two locations) – checked twice daily; interactive fountain (Centennial) – checked daily for operation and water quality; irrigation systems (29 locations)- checked 4 times weekly, empty trash and recycle cans – 3 times weekly; pick up of litter, debris, palm fronds, etc. – 3 times weekly or as needed due to high winds; playground equipment (6 locations) – checked weekly for safety; decorative fountains (4 locations) – checked weekly for operation; parking lot sweeping - weekly; shell parking lot maintenance (South Jetty) – weekly or as needed following most rainfall events; mowing (all locations) – once a week in rainy season/irrigated, every other week in dry season; tree trimming (all locations) – annually; parking lot striping (4 locations) – every 2 to 4 years; repairs to potholes, walkways, buildings/building systems, shelters, and other amenities – as needed.

★ Washington, Missouri

Special Mention: Jaycee's All-Abilities Playground

This new playground is a wonderful addition to the community. One third of the cost was donated by the Washington Jaycees. Now special needs children can play side-by-side with typically developing youngsters. The attractive, soft flooring and easily accessible play units are designed to let all children play safely.

Best Ideas: The Moving Wall – an honorable welcome home. Whether we were in favor of the Vietnam War nor not, our soldiers deserve better than they got. This idea was conceived by the VFW for their upcoming 75th anniversary of their organization in Washington, MO. The idea behind bringing the Moving Wall to Washington, MO was to honor, respect, and remember the members of the armed forces who lost their lives and those who were missing in action in the Vietnam War as a tribute to their courage and unselfish devotion to the United States of America. It also is to remember those who returned from Vietnam, sometimes to an indifferent or hostile American public. Visiting the wall is a way to finally welcome home Vietnam Veterans. This event is in memory of the 25 local service members whose names appear on the Moving Wall and the 2.7 million men and woman who served in the U.S. Military in Vietnam. There are 58,282 names of those who paid the ultimate price listed on the polished black wall. The Moving Wall is a 50% scaled replica of the Vietnam Memorial in Washington DC. Since the debut of the Moving Wall in October 1984, through September 2013, when it was in Washington, Mo it had visited 1,304 communities. The Friends of the Vietnam Veterans which not only includes VFW members but people who have the desire to make things right worked with the city of Washington and surrounding communities to make the idea a reality! Remember there are no noble wars, just noble warriors. God Bless our community and America.

★ Winter Park, Florida

Special Mention: Hannibal Square Heritage Center

The Hannibal Square Heritage Center tells the important history of the African-American influence on the development of Winter Park. Located in the historically black neighborhood adjacent to downtown, the Center is a unique experience relating the history of the community as told by its members through oral histories and photographs. For a number of years the area languished, then its prime location fueled development and gentrification, with significant loss of cultural landmarks and long-time residents. Today there exists a renewed vitality and vision as the Hannibal Square Heritage Center and its exhibitions and programs weave the stories of this proud neighborhood together into an inspiring example of what is possible through the blending of historic preservation with the visual arts.

Best Ideas: +The project undertaken to save the historic Capen House is a testament to the value that Winter Park residents place on their historic resources. The collaborative effort between the Albin Polasek Museum and Sculpture Garden, Casa Feliz (yet another preservation success story), and the Winter Park History Museum was a huge success. The ingenious plan to float the house across Lake Osceola to its new home adjacent to the Albin Polasek Museum and Sculpture Garden was a daunting feat, but the 129 year old residence seems quite at home at its new spot across the lake.

★ Wisconsin Rapids, Wisconsin

Special Mention: The Tribune Building Project

This project started when Incourage Community Foundation purchased a historic property along the Wisconsin River with the intent that residents would decide its future use. This project is about so much more than the design of the building; it's about energy, and the will of residents who believe in the future of this community.

Best Ideas: After many crime related incidents in Wisconsin Rapids Ward 1 District, Ward 1 Alderman, the Mayor, Police Chief, and the Planning and Zoning Director were contacted by residents with a serious concern for their neighborhoods. The Mayor held a meeting with city departments and residents at the City Hall to hear and address concerns and issues of the community.

An initiative was formed from these meetings directed from the Mayor's office called "RapidServes," part of the "Love Your Block" initiative that the city is a part of. On May 18, a community cleanup day was coordinated. T-shirts were provided, and 43 neighbors, city staff and community members met at the 8th Avenue Plaza in Wisconsin Rapids ready to help. Area businesses partnered in the initiative; rakes, trash bags, trimmers, and shovels were donated from Home Depot, Tractor Supply, and Ace Hardware. The effort received financial support from local businesses and food items were also donated to feed the volunteers. Businesses and residents came together to help clean up the community.

In all, 12 yards were raked and cleaned up. In addition, volunteers picked up tires, appliances, and garbage alongside residences. The best part was the community built an interest in taking the initiative to more neighborhoods. A fall cleanup was held in October with great success and the "Neighborhood Group" is now part of our group which meets monthly. The "Neighborhood Group" addresses concerns of blight in their neighborhoods and plans future cleanup efforts. The group is framed around the goals of education, advocacy and action. Cleanup works while the community gets a shot in the arm to create a visually appealing and safer area. We begin to see what is possible through a collective vision!

Giving to America in Bloom

Sponsorship opportunities are available at several levels. To make a gift or become a corporate sponsor, please contact us at aib@AmericaInBloom.org or 614-487-1117.

Join the Excitement - Register for 2015

Getting your community involved with America in Bloom is a great way to generate excitement and visible improvements. Start by attending our symposium in the fall, or simply sign up for the next program. Check for symposium and registration details, and sign up for our free e-newsletter at www.AmericaInBloom.org. **Each year, the registration deadline is February 28. Register by December 31 and get a complimentary copy of the "Best Ideas" book.**

Need more books?

Please contact the AIB office to order the Best Ideas book and more copies of this addendum or order online.

aib@AmericaInBloom.org   614-487-1117

www.AmericaInBloom.org

Thanks to Our Sponsor

Our gratitude to Mountaineer Mechanical Co. for sponsoring the printing of this addendum.

www.mountaineermechanical.com
800-905-4172

★ Wisconsin Rapids, Wisconsin

Special Mention: The Tribune Building Project

This project started when Incourage Community Foundation purchased a historic property along the Wisconsin River with the intent that residents would decide its future use. This project is about so much more than the design of the building; it's about energy, and the will of residents who believe in the future of this community.

Best Ideas: After many crime related incidents in Wisconsin Rapids Ward 1 District, Ward 1 Alderman, the Mayor, Police Chief, and the Planning and Zoning Director were contacted by residents with a serious concern for their neighborhoods. The Mayor held a meeting with city departments and residents at the City Hall to hear and address concerns and issues of the community.

An initiative was formed from these meetings directed from the Mayor's office called "RapidServes," part of the "Love Your Block" initiative that the city is a part of. On May 18, a community cleanup day was coordinated. T-shirts were provided, and 43 neighbors, city staff and community members met at the 8th Avenue Plaza in Wisconsin Rapids ready to help. Area businesses partnered in the initiative; rakes, trash bags, trimmers, and shovels were donated from Home Depot, Tractor Supply, and Ace Hardware. The effort received financial support from local businesses and food items were also donated to feed the volunteers. Businesses and residents came together to help clean up the community.

In all, 12 yards were raked and cleaned up. In addition, volunteers picked up tires, appliances, and garbage alongside residences. The best part was the community built an interest in taking the initiative to more neighborhoods. A fall cleanup was held in October with great success and the "Neighborhood Group" is now part of our group which meets monthly. The "Neighborhood Group" addresses concerns of blight in their neighborhoods and plans future cleanup efforts. The group is framed around the goals of education, advocacy and action. Cleanup works while the community gets a shot in the arm to create a visually appealing and safer area. We begin to see what is possible through a collective vision!

Giving to America in Bloom

Sponsorship opportunities are available at several levels. To make a gift or become a corporate sponsor, please contact us at aib@AmericaInBloom.org or 614-487-1117.

Join the Excitement - Register for 2015

Getting your community involved with America in Bloom is a great way to generate excitement and visible improvements. Start by attending our symposium in the fall, or simply sign up for the next program. Check for symposium and registration details, and sign up for our free e-newsletter at www.AmericaInBloom.org. **Each year, the registration deadline is February 28. Register by December 31 and get a complimentary copy of the "Best Ideas" book.**

Need more books?

Please contact the AIB office to order the Best Ideas book and more copies of this addendum or order online.

aib@AmericaInBloom.org   614-487-1117

www.AmericaInBloom.org

Thanks to Our Sponsor

Our gratitude to Mountaineer Mechanical Co. for sponsoring the printing of this addendum.

www.mountaineermechanical.com
800-905-4172

Morro Bay, CA

★ 2014 Judges

We appreciate the expertise and generous donation of time by our judges, who are all volunteers.

Jack Clasen -
  Chair, National Awards/
  Contest Committee

Evelyn Alemanni

Sue Amatangelo

Billy Butterfield*

Diane Clasen*

Linda Cromer

Bill Hahn*

Ed Hooker III

Dwight Lund*

Marlborough Packard

Stephen Pategas

Leslie Pittenger

Alex Pearl

Bruce Riggs

Melanie Riggs

Karin Rindal

Susie Stratton

Jim Sutton

Barbara Vincentsen

Katy Moss Warner

Diana K. Weiner*

* = alternate for 2014

**This annual edition is
dedicated to our
America in Bloom
family, working
together to make
America a better
place to live,
one community
at a time.**

Lexington, KY